MASTERING LFCS: YOUR GATEWAY TO LINUX CERTIFICATION

A Comprehensive Guide for LFCS Exam
Preparation and Linux System Administration

Ghada Atef

To all the aspiring Linux enthusiasts and system administrators, who tirelessly delve into the depths of code, seeking knowledge and understanding. May this book light your path towards mastery and success.

"In the world of technology, simplicity often stems from mastery. Here's to mastering the art of simplicity through Linux."

ANONYMOUS

CONTENTS

PREFACE

In the ever-evolving world of technology, Linux has established itself as a robust and reliable operating system, powering millions of servers worldwide and offering a versatile platform for developers and system administrators alike. The Linux Foundation Certified System Administrator (LFCS) certification is a testament to an individual's proficiency in managing this powerful tool.

"Mastering LFCS: Your Gateway to Linux Certification" is designed to be a comprehensive guide for those preparing for the LFCS exam, as well as for those seeking to enhance their understanding of Linux system administration. This book is the culmination of countless hours of research, practical experience, and dedication to bringing the most relevant and up-to-date information to the reader.

The journey to mastering Linux is not always easy, but it is undoubtedly rewarding. This book aims to be your companion on this journey, providing clear explanations, practical examples, and insights drawn from real-world scenarios. Whether you're a seasoned system administrator looking to validate your skills with certification, or a newcomer to the Linux world, this book is designed with you in mind.

I hope that "Mastering LFCS: Your Gateway to Linux Certification" serves not just as a study guide, but also as a valuable reference that you will return to throughout your Linux journey. Here's to your success in the LFCS exam and beyond!

PROLOGUE

In the vast universe of technology, Linux stands as a beacon of power, flexibility, and control. It is an operating system that has not only stood the test of time but has also adapted and evolved, becoming an essential tool in the arsenal of millions of developers and system administrators worldwide.

The Linux Foundation Certified System Administrator (LFCS) certification is a significant milestone on the path of mastering Linux, a testament to the holder's understanding and proficiency in this powerful operating system.

"Mastering LFCS: Your Gateway to Linux Certification" is more than just a book; it is a journey into the heart of Linux. This journey may be challenging, filled with complex concepts and new ideas, but it is one that promises great rewards. With every page, you will find yourself delving deeper into the world of Linux, unraveling its intricacies, and gaining a deeper understanding of the operating system.

This book is designed to be your guide on this journey, providing a comprehensive path towards preparing for the LFCS exam and mastering Linux system administration. It is a path that requires dedication, perseverance, and a thirst for knowledge.

As you embark on this journey, remember that every master

was once a beginner, every expert started as a novice, and every Linux guru began with a single command. Here's to your journey towards mastering LFCS and beyond!

Ghada Atef

CONTACT ME

Thank you for grabbing a copy of my book **Mastering LFCS: Your Gateway to Linux Certification!** I hope you found the book informative and helpful on your journey.

If you have any questions, comments, or suggestions, please feel free to contact me through the following channels:

Email: [linux.expert.eg@gmail.com]

Social Media:

[https://www.linkedin.com/in/ghada-atef/]

I strive to respond to all inquiries within 48 hours.

I am always looking for ways to improve my work, so your feedback is greatly appreciated. Thank you for helping me make this book the best it can be!

CHAPTER 1: OPERATIONS DEPLOYMENT

Introduction to Linux System Administration

Overview

This section serves as an introduction to Linux System Administration, laying the foundation for the subsequent sections. It covers essential concepts, terminology, and basic commands that are fundamental for aspiring Linux administrators.

Understanding the Linux Operating System

Linux, at its core, is an open-source Unix-like operating system kernel. Understanding its architecture, file structure, and the philosophy behind it is crucial for effective system administration.

Key Concepts:

- **Kernel:** The core of the operating system that interacts with the hardware.
- **Shell:** The interface between the user and the kernel, allowing command execution.
- **File System Hierarchy:** Hierarchical structure organizing files and directories.

Getting Started with Basic Commands

Before diving into advanced system administration tasks, it's important to be familiar with fundamental commands. These commands form the building blocks for managing files, directories, and user interactions.

Basic Commands:

1. **pwd:** Print the current working directory.

pwd

2. **ls:** List directory contents.

ls

3. **cd:** Change the current directory.

cd /path/to/directory

4. **mkdir:** Create a new directory.

mkdir new_directory

5. **cp:** Copy files or directories.

cp source_file destination

6. **mv:** Move or rename files or directories.

mv old_name new_name

7. **rm:** Remove files or directories.

rm file_name

Practical Exercise:

Execute the following commands in your Linux environment and observe the changes:

$ cd ~

$ pwd

$ ls

$ mkdir test_directory

$ touch file.txt

$ ls

$ cp file.txt test_directory

$ ls test_directory

The Role of a Linux System Administrator

Understanding the responsibilities of a Linux system administrator is essential. It involves managing users, configuring system settings, ensuring security, and troubleshooting issues.

Key Responsibilities:

- User and Group Management
- System Configuration
- Security Management
- Troubleshooting

Setting the Stage for Advanced Topics

This chapter sets the stage for the advanced topics covered in subsequent chapters. Building a strong foundation with basic commands and concepts is key to becoming a proficient Linux system administrator.

Section 1: Manage System Services with SysVinit, Systemd, and Upstart

Overview

This section delves into SysVinit, Systemd, and Upstart, elucidating their architectures, command-line tools, configuration files, and service management techniques. Understanding the differences and advantages of each is essential for success in LFCS.

SysVinit

SysVinit, an abbreviation for System V initialization, serves as the traditional init system for Unix-like operating systems. It operates on the concept of runlevels, representing distinct states of the system.

- Architecture:

SysVinit utilizes a collection of scripts in `/etc/init.d/` to initiate or halt services. These scripts are symbolically linked to various runlevel directories, such as `/etc/rc.d/rc3.d/` for runlevel 3.

- Command-line tools:

The primary command for service management is `service`, invoked as `service <service-name> <command>`, where `<command>` can be start, stop, restart, etc.

- Configuration files:

The principal configuration file is `/etc/inittab`, defining the default runlevel and managing gettys.

Start a service

```
$ sudo service httpd start
```

Stop a service
```
$ sudo service httpd stop
```

Systemd

Systemd, a modern init system adopted by many Linux distributions, employs a dependency-based model and initiates services in parallel for optimized boot speed.

- Architecture:

Systemd relies on unit files (service, socket, device, mount, etc.) stored in `/usr/lib/systemd/system/` and `/etc/systemd/system/`.

- Command-line tools:

Service management is executed using the `systemctl` command, as in `systemctl <command> <service-name>`.

- Configuration files:

Each service is defined by a unit file, e.g., `/usr/lib/systemd/system/httpd.service`, with the ability to override it using a file of the same name in `/etc/systemd/system/`.

Start a service
```
$ sudo systemctl start httpd
```

Enable a service to start on boot
```
$ sudo systemctl enable httpd
```

Upstart

Upstart, an event-based init system designed for asynchronous task handling, enhances boot times.

- Architecture:

Upstart utilizes job files located in `/etc/init/` to articulate services.

- Command-line tools:

Service management involves the use of either the `initctl` or `service` command.

- Configuration files:

Each service is defined by a job file, e.g., `/etc/init/httpd.conf`.

Start a service

```
$ sudo initctl start httpd
```

Stop a service

```
$ sudo initctl stop httpd
```

Differences and Advantages

- SysVinit:

Simple and understandable, but lacks dependency handling and does not support parallel service startup.

- Systemd:

Powerful and flexible, offering features like cgroups for resource control, parallel startup, and detailed logging with `journalctl`.

Its complexity can be a challenge.

- Upstart:

Strikes a balance with its event-driven model, allowing for parallel and asynchronous task handling. However, it is less common and has been largely replaced by Systemd in many distributions.

Section 2: Package Management with Yum, Dnf, RPM, Apt, Dpkg, Aptitude, and Zypper

Overview

This section illuminates Yum, Dnf, RPM, Apt, Dpkg, Aptitude, and Zypper, unraveling their roles, commands, and methodologies for adept software management.

Yum

Yum (Yellowdog Updater, Modified) stands as a package manager prominent in RPM-based Linux systems, such as CentOS and older Fedora versions.

- Role:

Facilitates the automated resolution of dependencies for RPM packages.

- Commands:

   - Install: `yum install <package>`

   - Remove: `yum remove <package>`

   - Update: `yum update <package>`

Dnf

Dnf (Dandified Yum), the evolution of Yum, is employed in modern Fedora versions and other RPM-based systems.

- Role:

Similar to Yum but excels in performance and dependency resolution.

- Commands:
  - Install: `dnf install <package>`
  - Remove: `dnf remove <package>`
  - Update: `dnf update <package>`

RPM

RPM Package Manager, a low-level tool in RPM-based systems, focuses on managing individual RPM packages but does not handle dependencies.

- Commands:
  - Install: `rpm -i <package.rpm>`
  - Remove: `rpm -e <package>`
  - Update: `rpm -U <package.rpm>`

Apt

Apt (Advanced Package Tool) emerges as a high-level package manager in Debian-based systems like Ubuntu.

- Role:

Manages automatic resolution of dependencies for DEB packages.

- Commands:
  - Install: `apt install <package>`
  - Remove: `apt remove <package>`
  - Update: `apt update && apt upgrade`

Dpkg

Dpkg, a low-level package manager in Debian-based systems,

concentrates on managing individual DEB packages without handling dependencies.

- Commands:
  - Install: `dpkg -i <package.deb>`
  - Remove: `dpkg -r <package>`

Aptitude

Aptitude, a text-based interface for Apt, brings additional features to the table.

- Role:

Resembles Apt but offers a user-friendly text interface.

- Commands:
  - Install: `aptitude install <package>`
  - Remove: `aptitude remove <package>`
  - Update: `aptitude update && aptitude upgrade`

Zypper

Zypper, a command-line package manager for openSUSE and SLES, adeptly handles automatic dependency resolution for RPM packages.

- Commands:
  - Install: `zypper install <package>`
  - Remove: `zypper remove <package>`
  - Update: `zypper update <package>`

Comparison

- Yum/Dnf/Zypper:

Similar trio providing automatic dependency resolution for RPM packages. Dnf, a modern successor, outshines Yum in performance. Zypper is tailored for openSUSE/SLES.

- RPM:

Low-level tool lacking dependency handling, suitable for installing individual packages.

- Apt/Aptitude:

Found in Debian-based systems, with Aptitude offering additional features through a text interface.

- Dpkg:

Low-level tool similar to RPM but tailored for DEB packages in Debian-based systems.

Section 3: Set Kernel Runtime Parameters in Linux

Overview

In this section, we will explore the essential task of configuring kernel runtime parameters in Linux, a critical aspect of system administration for LFCS learners.

Understanding Kernel Parameters

Kernel parameters serve as critical settings that govern the behavior of the Linux kernel, providing system administrators with the ability to fine-tune system performance and functionality.

Viewing and Modifying Kernel Parameters

/proc Filesystem

The /proc filesystem serves as a virtual interface to kernel data structures, housing kernel parameters under /proc/sys/. This allows for efficient viewing and modification.

- Viewing:

```
cat /proc/sys/fs/file-max
```

Example: View the maximum number of file handles.

- Modifying:

```
echo 200000 > /proc/sys/fs/file-max
```

Example: Change the maximum number of file handles to 200,000.

sysctl Utility

The sysctl utility offers a more user-friendly approach to handle kernel parameters, operating on those located under /proc/sys/.

- Viewing:

sysctl fs.file-max

Example: View the maximum number of file handles using sysctl.

- Modifying:

sysctl -w fs.file-max=200000

Example: Modify the maximum number of file handles to 200,000 using sysctl.

Common Kernel Parameters

Here are some frequently encountered kernel parameters with typical values:

- fs.file-max:

    - Description: Maximum number of file handles.

    - Typical Values: Tens or hundreds of thousands.

- net.ipv4.ip_forward:

    - Description: Controls IP forwarding.

    - Typical Values: 0 (off) or 1 (on).

- kernel.shmmax:

    - Description: Maximum size of shared memory segments.

    - Typical Values: Depends on your system's RAM.

Making Changes Persistent

Changes made using echo or sysctl -w are not persistent and will be lost on reboot. To ensure persistence, add them to the configuration files in /etc/sysctl.conf or a file under /etc/sysctl.d/.

- Example:

To make the fs.file-max change persistent, add the following line to /etc/sysctl.conf:

fs.file-max = 200000

Then load the changes with:

sysctl -p

Example: Make the fs.file-max change persistent in the sysctl configuration.

Section 4: Managing and Configuring Virtual Machines and Containers

Overview

In this section, we will explore the dynamic realms of virtual machines (VMs) and containers, fundamental components for LFCS learners involved in system administration.

Virtualization vs Containerization

Virtualization

Virtualization involves running multiple operating systems on a single physical system. Each operating system runs inside a virtual machine (VM), which emulates a complete hardware system, encompassing the processor to the network card.

Containerization

Containerization, on the other hand, involves running multiple applications on a single operating system, with each application operating within a separate container. Containers share the host system's OS kernel but run in isolated user spaces.

Virtual Machines

KVM/QEMU

KVM (Kernel-based Virtual Machine) is a Linux kernel module enabling the kernel to function as a hypervisor. QEMU is an open-source machine emulator and virtualizer that pairs seamlessly with KVM.

- Create a VM:

```
qemu-img create -f qcow2 myvm.img 20G
qemu-system-x86_64 -hda myvm.img -boot d -cdrom ubuntu.iso
```

Example: Create a VM image and start a VM with an Ubuntu ISO.

- Start/Stop a VM:

```
virsh start myvm
virsh shutdown myvm
```

Example: Start and stop a VM using virsh.

- Manage VMs:

```
virsh list
virsh console myvm
```

Example: List running VMs and connect to a VM using virsh.

VirtualBox

VirtualBox is a versatile virtualization product for x86 and AMD64/Intel64 architectures.

- Create a VM:

```
VBoxManage createvm --name myvm --ostype Linux_64 --register
```

Example: Create a VM using VBoxManage.

- Start/Stop a VM:

```
VBoxManage startvm myvm
VBoxManage controlvm myvm poweroff
```

Example: Start and stop a VM using VBoxManage.

- Manage VMs:

VBoxManage list vms

Example: List all VMs using VBoxManage.

Containers

Docker

Docker is a platform utilizing OS-level virtualization to deliver software in containers.

- Create a container:

docker run -d --name mycontainer ubuntu:latest

Example: Create a Docker container using the docker run command.

- Start/Stop a container:

docker start mycontainer

docker stop mycontainer

Example: Start and stop a Docker container.

- Manage containers:

docker ps

Example: List all running Docker containers.

Podman

Podman is a daemonless container engine for developing, managing, and running OCI Containers on Linux systems.

- Create a container:

podman run -d --name mypodmancontainer ubuntu:latest

Example: Create a Podman container using the podman run command.

- Start/Stop a container:

podman start mypodmancontainer

podman stop mypodmancontainer

Example: Start and stop a Podman container.

- Manage containers:

podman ps

Example: List all running Podman containers.

Security Considerations

When dealing with VMs and containers, prioritize security. Keep VMs and containers updated with the latest security patches, limit open ports, and use secure, private networks when possible.

Challenges

One significant challenge with VMs and containers is resource management. VMs can be resource-intensive, while containers, though more lightweight, may still consume substantial resources if not appropriately managed.

Section 5: SELinux and AppArmor

Overview

In this section, we will explore the realm of Linux security modules, with a focus on SELinux and AppArmor, crucial components for LFCS learners in mastering Linux security.

SELinux

SELinux (Security-Enhanced Linux) is a mandatory access control (MAC) security mechanism integrated into the kernel. Its primary function is to limit the permissions of applications to the minimum necessary for correct operation.

- Enable/Disable:

getenforce

Example: Check if SELinux is enabled.

setenforce 0   # Permissive mode

setenforce 1   # Enforcing mode (temporary)

Example: Temporarily change SELinux mode.

To make the change permanent, modify the `SELINUX=` line in `/etc/selinux/config`.

- Configuration:

SELinux policies reside in `/etc/selinux/`, with the main configuration file at `/etc/selinux/config`.

- Management:

semanage

Example: Use `semanage` to configure certain elements of SELinux policy without modifying or recompiling policy sources.

sestatus

Example: Check SELinux status.

AppArmor

AppArmor (Application Armor) is a Linux Security Module (LSM) that safeguards the operating system by applying profiles to individual applications. Unlike SELinux, it employs a path-based approach and does not use labels.

- Enable/Disable:

systemctl start apparmor

systemctl stop apparmor

Example: Use `systemctl` to start or stop AppArmor.

- Configuration:

AppArmor profiles are located in `/etc/apparmor.d/`, with each profile represented as a file in this directory.

- Management:

sudo aa-enforce /etc/apparmor.d/usr.bin.firefox

Example: Use `aa-enforce` to set an AppArmor profile to enforce mode.

sudo aa-complain /etc/apparmor.d/usr.bin.firefox

Example: Use `aa-complain` to set an AppArmor profile to complain mode.

Comparison

SELinux and AppArmor share the goal of enhancing security but adopt different approaches. SELinux provides fine-grained controls, suitable for high-security environments. AppArmor, path-based and easier to set up, is well-suited for common use cases.

Challenges and Best Practices

Working with SELinux and AppArmor can be challenging due to policy complexity. It's crucial to thoroughly test changes in a non-production environment before deployment. Utilize tools like `audit2why` (part of `policycoreutils-python-utils` package) to understand SELinux denials and `aa-logprof` to update AppArmor profiles based on log events.

CHAPTER 2: NETWORKING

Section 1: Setup Network Share (Samba & NFS) File-Systems

Overview

In this section, we will explore the configuration of network shares using Samba and NFS. These protocols enable seamless file sharing and access across different operating systems, specifically between Unix/Linux systems and Windows clients.

Samba

Samba Overview:

Samba is a free software re-implementation of the SMB networking protocol. It facilitates file and print services from Unix/Linux systems to Windows clients.

Configuration Steps:

1. Install Samba: Use the command `sudo apt-get install samba` on Debian-based systems.

2. Configure Samba: Modify the main configuration file at `/etc/samba/smb.conf` to define shares, set up user authentication, and configure access control. Example configuration:

```
[share]
path = /path/to/share
valid users = user1 user2
read only = no
```

3. Manage Samba Users: Utilize `smbpasswd` to add users and manage passwords. For instance, to add a new user: `sudo

smbpasswd -a username`.

4. Start the Samba Service: Launch the Samba service with `sudo service smbd start`.

Integration with Windows Clients:

Windows clients can access Samba shares by entering the server's IP address in the format `\\server-ip\share-name` in the File Explorer.

NFS

NFS Overview:

Network File System (NFS) is a distributed file system protocol enabling users on client computers to access files over a network as if they were local.

Configuration Steps:

1. Install NFS: Execute `sudo apt-get install nfs-kernel-server` on Debian-based systems.

2. Configure NFS: Modify the main configuration file at `/etc/exports` to define exported directories and set permissions. Example configuration:

/path/to/export   client1(rw,sync,no_subtree_check) client2(ro,sync,no_subtree_check)

3. Export the Shares: Use `sudo exportfs -a` to export the shares.

4. Start the NFS Service: Launch the NFS service with `sudo service nfs-kernel-server start`.

Mounting NFS Shares:

On the client side, use the `mount` command to mount NFS shares:

```
sudo mount -t nfs server:/path/to/export /path/to/local/mountpoint
```

Troubleshooting Tips:

- Use `testparm` to check Samba configuration for errors.

- On the client side, employ `showmount -e server` to list exported NFS shares.

- Check logs (`/var/log/samba/` for Samba, `/var/log/syslog` for NFS) for error messages.

Best Practices:

- Restrict access to shares to trusted users and networks.

- Implement strong passwords for Samba users.

- Regularly update Samba and NFS packages for the latest security updates.

Section 2: Setting Up Network Services NFS, Apache, Squid +SquidGuard, Postfix+Dovecot

Overview

This section explores the setup of essential Linux network services, specifically focusing on NFS, Apache, Squid with SquidGuard, and Postfix with Dovecot. These services play crucial roles in networking, file sharing, web hosting, proxy services, and email management.

NFS (Network File System)

NFS Overview:

NFS facilitates the sharing of directories and files across a network. In an NFS setup, the server shares a part of its file system, allowing clients to mount this share and access files as if they were local.

Installation:

To install NFS on a Debian-based system, use the command:

sudo apt-get install nfs-kernel-server

Configuration:

Modify the main configuration file at `/etc/exports` to define directories to export and set permissions. Example configuration:

*/path/to/export   client1(rw,sync,no_subtree_check)
client2(ro,sync,no_subtree_check)*

Management:

Export the shares with:

sudo exportfs -a

Start the NFS service with:

sudo service nfs-kernel-server start

Apache

Apache Overview:

Apache is widely used as a web server software, serving files over the HTTP protocol.

Installation:

Install Apache on Debian-based systems using:

sudo apt-get install apache2

Configuration:

The main configuration file is `/etc/apache2/apache2.conf`, and virtual host files are located in `/etc/apache2/sites-available/`.

Management:

Start the Apache service with:

sudo service apache2 start

Squid with SquidGuard

Squid Overview:

Squid functions as a caching proxy for the web, and SquidGuard is a URL redirector used to apply blacklists with the proxy.

Installation:

Install Squid and SquidGuard on Debian-based systems using:

sudo apt-get install squid squidguard

Configuration:

The main configuration file for Squid is `/etc/squid/squid.conf`, and for SquidGuard, it's `/etc/squidguard/squidGuard.conf`.

Management:

Start the Squid service with:

sudo service squid start

Postfix with Dovecot

Postfix and Dovecot Overview:

Postfix serves as a free and open-source mail transfer agent, while Dovecot is an open-source IMAP and POP3 server.

Installation:

Install Postfix and Dovecot on Debian-based systems using:

sudo apt-get install postfix dovecot-imapd

Configuration:

The main configuration file for Postfix is `/etc/postfix/main.cf`, and for Dovecot, it's `/etc/dovecot/dovecot.conf`.

Management:

Start the Postfix and Dovecot services with:

sudo service postfix start

sudo service dovecot start

Section 3: Setup Recursive Caching DNS Server

Overview

This section explores the setup of a recursive caching DNS server, focusing on BIND (Berkeley Internet Name Domain). Understanding the significance of DNS and the advantages of using a recursive caching DNS server is crucial for effective network management.

Significance of DNS

DNS Overview:

DNS is a hierarchical and decentralized naming system for computers, services, or resources connected to the Internet or private networks. It translates human-friendly domain names into numerical IP addresses, essential for locating and identifying computer services and devices.

Advantages of a Recursive Caching DNS Server

A. Recursion:

A recursive caching DNS server can query other DNS servers on behalf of the requesting client, providing a seamless experience. This involves resolving a domain name by traversing the DNS hierarchy.

B. Caching:

The server stores (caches) DNS query results for a specified period, enhancing the speed of subsequent requests for the same domain name.

Setting Up a Recursive Caching DNS Server

Using BIND:

BIND is chosen for its widespread use on the internet.

1. Install BIND:

On a Debian-based system, install BIND with:

```
sudo apt-get install bind9
```

2. Configure BIND:

Modify the main configuration file at `/etc/bind/named.conf.options`. Set options such as `listen-on` (specifying IP addresses to listen on), `allow-query` (specifying who can query your DNS server), and `recursion` (enabling or disabling recursion).

Example Configuration:

```
bind
 options {
   listen-on { 192.168.1.1; };
   allow-query { localhost; 192.168.1.0/24; };
   recursion yes;
   forwarders {
     8.8.8.8;
     8.8.4.4;
   };
 };
```

This example sets the DNS server to listen on IP 192.168.1.1, allows queries from the local network, enables recursion, and forwards queries to Google's DNS servers.

3. Start the BIND Service:

Launch the BIND service with:

sudo service bind9 start

Troubleshooting Tips

- Use `dig` or `nslookup` to test your DNS server.

- Check logs (`/var/log/syslog`) for any error messages.

- Use `named-checkconf` to check your BIND configuration for errors.

Best Practices

- Restrict access to your DNS server to trusted networks.

- Regularly update your BIND package to get the latest security updates.

Section 4: Static and Dynamic Routing

Overview

This section explores the concepts of static and dynamic routing, fundamental for effective network management.

Static Routing

A. Definition:

Static routing involves routers using manually-configured routing entries, bypassing dynamic routing traffic information.

B. Configuration:

In Linux, static routes can be added using the `ip` command. For instance, to add a route to the `192.168.1.0/24` network via the gateway at `192.168.0.1`:

```
sudo ip route add 192.168.1.0/24 via 192.168.0.1
```

C. Usage:

Static routing is simple without extra protocol overhead. However, it's impractical for large, changing networks due to manual route updates.

Dynamic Routing

A. Definition:

Dynamic routing enables routers to adapt to real-time logical network changes. Common protocols include OSPF and BGP.

B. OSPF (Open Shortest Path First):

OSPF is a link-state routing protocol using the Dijkstra algorithm for the shortest path calculation. Configure OSPF using the Quagga suite in Linux with the main configuration file at `/etc/quagga/ospfd.conf`.

C. BGP (Border Gateway Protocol):

BGP is a path-vector protocol widely used for routing among autonomous systems on the internet. Configure BGP using the Quagga suite with the main configuration file at `/etc/quagga/bgpd.conf`.

D. Advantages:

Dynamic routing adapts to network changes automatically, making it suitable for large, evolving networks.

Troubleshooting and Best Practices

A. Troubleshooting:

1. Use `ip route` to view the routing table.

2. Employ `ping` and `traceroute` to test connectivity and path selection.

3. Regularly check configuration files for errors.

B. Best Practices:

For dynamic routing, ensure all routers share the same routing protocol and parameters.

Section 5: Configure IPv4 and IPv6 Networking and Hostname Resolution

Overview

This section delves into IPv4 and IPv6 networking, emphasizing addressing, network interface configuration, routing tables, hostname resolution methods, and associated troubleshooting tips and best practices.

IPv4 and IPv6 Addressing

A. IPv4 Addressing:

IPv4 utilizes 32-bit addresses, offering 4.3 billion unique addresses. Example IPv4 address: `192.168.1.1`.

B. IPv6 Addressing:

IPv6 employs 128-bit addresses, accommodating an immense number of unique addresses. Example IPv6 address: `2001:0db8:85a3:0000:0000:8a2e:0370:7334`.

Main Difference:

IPv6 addresses the IPv4 address exhaustion problem with its increased address space.

Configuring Network Interfaces

A. Using the `ip` command:

To set a static IP address using the `ip` command:

For IPv4

sudo ip addr add 192.168.1.100/24 dev eth0

For IPv6

sudo ip -6 addr add 2001:db8::100/64 dev eth0

B. Editing the network configuration file:

Configure network interfaces by editing `/etc/network/interfaces`.

Managing Routing Tables

Use the `ip` command to manage routing tables. Example for adding a default gateway:

For IPv4

sudo ip route add default via 192.168.1.1

For IPv6

sudo ip -6 route add default via 2001:db8::1

Hostname Resolution

Hostname resolution translates a hostname into an IP address through methods like `/etc/hosts`, DNS, etc.

A. /etc/hosts:

A simple method containing lines of text with an IP address followed by one or more hostnames.

B. DNS (Domain Name System):

A hierarchical and decentralized naming system for computers, services, or resources connected to the Internet or a private network.

Configuring Hostname-Related Settings

Set the hostname using the `hostname` command or by editing `/etc/hostname`.

Troubleshooting Tips

- Use `ping` and `traceroute` to test network connectivity.

- Employ `dig` or `nslookup` to test DNS resolution.

- Check logs (`/var/log/syslog`) for error messages.

Best Practices

- Use static IPs for servers.

- Utilize DNS for hostname resolution in large networks.

- Regularly update the system for the latest security updates.

Section 6: Configure Bonding and Bridge Devices

Overview

This section explores network bonding and bridge devices in Linux networking, highlighting the setup, configuration, bonding modes, and bridging for efficient network management.

Bonding

A. Definition:

Network bonding aggregates multiple network interfaces into a single logical interface, enhancing throughput and providing redundancy against link failures.

B. Setup:

1. Install ifenslave:

On a Debian-based system, install ifenslave using:

```
sudo apt-get install ifenslave
```

2. Configure bonding:

Modify the main configuration file at `` `/etc/network/interfaces` ``. Define the bond interface, and add physical interfaces to it.

Example Configuration:

```
auto bond0
iface bond0 inet static
    address 192.168.1.10
    netmask 255.255.255.0
    gateway 192.168.1.1
```

> *bond-slaves eth0 eth1*
> *bond-mode balance-rr*
> *bond-miimon 100*

3. Start the bond interface:

Use:

sudo ifup bond0

C. Bonding Modes:

Several bonding modes distribute traffic differently, including:

- balance-rr (Round-robin): Sequential packet transmission on each slave interface.

- active-backup: Only one slave interface active; another takes over if one fails.

- balance-xor: Outgoing interface selected based on XOR operation on MAC addresses.

- broadcast: All traffic transmitted on all slave interfaces.

- 802.3ad (IEEE 802.3ad Dynamic link aggregation): Aggregation groups sharing the same speed and duplex settings.

Bridging

A. Definition:

A network bridge is a Link Layer device forwarding traffic between networks based on MAC addresses, used to segment larger networks.

B. Setup:

1. Install bridge-utils:

On a Debian-based system, install bridge-utils using:

sudo apt-get install bridge-utils

2. Configure bridging:

Modify the main configuration file at `/etc/network/interfaces`. Define the bridge interface and add physical (or bond) interfaces to it.

Example Configuration:

```
auto br0
iface br0 inet static
    address 192.168.1.10
    netmask 255.255.255.0
    gateway 192.168.1.1
    bridge_ports eth0 eth1
```

3. Start the bridge interface:

Use:

sudo ifup br0

Troubleshooting Tips

- Use `ip addr` and `ip link` to check interface status.
- Check logs (`/var/log/syslog`) for error messages.

Best Practices

- Utilize static IP addresses for bond and bridge interfaces.
- Regularly update the system for the latest security updates.

CHAPTER 3: STORAGE

Section 1: Partitioning Storage Devices, Formatting Filesystems, and Configuring Swap Partitions

Overview

This section, focuses on Partitioning Storage Devices, Formatting Filesystems, and Configuring Swap Partitions.

Partitioning Storage Devices

A. Definition:

Partitioning involves dividing a physical storage device into smaller logical pieces called partitions.

B. Example:

To create a partition, use:

fdisk /dev/sdX

In this command, replace `/dev/sdX` with the actual storage device you intend to partition.

Formatting Filesystems

A. Requirement:

After creating a partition, it needs formatting with a filesystem.

B. Example (ext4):

To format a partition with the ext4 filesystem, use:

mkfs.ext4 /dev/sdXY

Replace `/dev/sdXY` with the specific partition you created.

Configuring Swap Partitions

A. Purpose:

Swap partitions offer additional memory resources to the system.

B. Example:

1. Create a swap partition with:

fdisk /dev/sdX

Designate the partition type as swap (usually type 82) when prompted.

2. Make the swap partition with:

mkswap /dev/sdXY

Replace ` /dev/sdXY ` with the designated swap partition.

System Configuration:

Each step in this process contributes to system configuration by organizing storage devices, preparing them for data storage, and enhancing memory resources as needed.

Section 2: Assembling Partitions as RAID Devices

Overview

This section, focuse on Assembling Partitions as RAID Devices, where RAID (Redundant Array of Independent Disks) configurations are explored for enhanced data reliability and performance.

RAID (Redundant Array of Independent Disks)

A. Definition:

RAID is a data storage method that distributes data across multiple disks to protect against drive failure. Different RAID levels offer varying balances between performance, data redundancy, and cost.

B. RAID Levels:

1. RAID 0 (Striping):

   - Splits data evenly across disks with no parity information.

   - Intended for increased performance, lacks data protection.

2. RAID 1 (Mirroring):

   - Duplicates data on two or more disks.

   - Provides data protection by duplicating all data from one drive to another.

3. RAID 5:

   - Distributes parity along with data, requires at least three disks.

   - Offers better performance than RAID 1.

4. RAID 6:

- Similar to RAID 5 but includes a second parity block for extra fault tolerance.

5. RAID 10:

- Combines RAID 1 and RAID 0.

- Provides redundancy of RAID 1 along with increased performance of RAID 0.

Assembling Partitions as RAID Devices

A. Process:

Assembling partitions into RAID devices involves the following steps.

1. Create a New Array using mdadm:

- If a partition has been formatted or part of another RAID array, confirm the creation of a new array.

- Example for creating a RAID 5 array with three devices and one spare device:

```
mdadm --create --verbose /dev/md0 --level=5 --raid-devices=3 /dev/sdb1 /dev/sdc1 /dev/sdd1 --spare-devices=1 /dev/sde1
```

- `/dev/md0`: RAID device to create.

- `--level=5`: Specifies RAID 5.

- `--raid-devices=3`: Three active devices in the array.

- `/dev/sdb1 /dev/sdc1 /dev/sdd1`: Active devices.

- `--spare-devices=1`: Specifies one spare device.

- `/dev/sde1`: Spare device.

B. Importance:

Understanding RAID concepts and procedures is crucial for LFCS and effective system administration. RAID configurations enhance data reliability and performance through data redundancy and distribution across multiple disks.

Section 3: Manage and Create LVM Partitions

Overview

This section, focuse on managing and creating LVM (Logical Volume Manager) partitions. LVM is a device mapper framework providing logical volume management for the Linux kernel, offering flexibility, performance improvement, and snapshot features.

Logical Volume Manager (LVM)

A. Definition:

LVM is a device mapper framework facilitating logical volume management for large disk drives. A "volume" refers to a disk drive or its partition.

B. Advantages:

1. Flexibility:

- LVM partitions can be resized, providing flexibility.

2. Performance:

- Performance improvement with striping.

3. Snapshots:

- LVM offers a snapshot feature, beneficial for backups.

Creating LVM Partitions

A. Process:

Creating LVM partitions involves several steps.

1. Creating Physical Volumes:

- Physical volumes are regular storage devices. Example:

pvcreate /dev/sdX

2. Creating Volume Groups:

- A volume group is a pool of disk space from one or more physical volumes. Example:

vgcreate volume_group_name /dev/sdX

3. Creating Logical Volumes:

- A logical volume is a portion of a volume group's disk space. Example:

lvcreate --size size --name logical_volume_name volume_group_name

4. Creating File Systems on Logical Volumes:

- After creating a logical volume, create a filesystem before mounting and using it. Example:

mkfs.ext4 /dev/volume_group_name/logical_volume_name

B. Considerations and Best Practices:

1. Partition Sizes:

- Plan carefully; while LVM partitions are resizable, resizing can be time-consuming and carry a risk of data loss.

2. Monitoring Logical Volumes:

- Regularly monitor usage to prevent space exhaustion.

3. LVM Snapshot Feature:

- Utilize LVM snapshots for backups, creating point-in-time images for secure file system backups.

Section 4: Configuring NFS Shares with Autofs

Overview

Section 4 delves into configuring NFS (Network File System) Shares using Autofs. NFS is a distributed file system protocol enabling network access to files, and Autofs is an automount daemon dynamically managing mount points for enhanced performance.

Network File System (NFS)

A. Definition:

NFS is a distributed file system protocol facilitating network access to files as if they were on local storage. It enables file system sharing between Linux or UNIX systems over a network.

Autofs

A. Definition:

Autofs is an automount daemon dynamically managing mount points, mounting them only when accessed. It optimizes bandwidth usage and outperforms static mounts controlled by /etc/fstab.

B. Advantages:

1. Dynamic Mounting:

- Mounts are dynamically created upon access, conserving bandwidth.

2. Performance:

- Offers better performance compared to static mounts.

Configuring NFS Shares Using Autofs

A. Steps:

1. Creating the Master Map File:

- Autofs uses /etc/auto.master to identify defined mount points. Each line in this file specifies a mount point and a separate map file defining file systems.

2. Creating the Map File:

- The map file, like /etc/auto.misc, defines mount points and includes fields for the mount point, the map file's location, and optional information such as a timeout value.

3. Starting the Autofs Service:

- Start the autofs service with `/sbin/service autofs restart` after configuring the necessary files.

4. Verifying Active Mount Points:

- Use `/sbin/service autofs status` to verify active mount points.

B. Example:

Add the following line to auto.master:

/test /etc/auto.misc --timeout 30

Add the following line to /etc/auto.misc:

autofstest -rw,soft,intr,rsize=8192,wsize=8192 client.example.com:/ afstest

- In this example, /test is the mount point, /etc/auto.misc is the map file location, and --timeout 30 is an optional field with a timeout set to 30 seconds.

C. Considerations and Best Practices:

1. Mount Point Planning:

- Plan mount points carefully, ensuring they align with the system's file hierarchy.

2. Monitoring Usage:

- Regularly monitor mount point usage to prevent space exhaustion.

3. Autofs Timeout Feature:

- Utilize the Autofs timeout feature to automatically unmount file systems after inactivity, conserving system resources.

Section 5: Encrypted Filesystems and Swap Space

Overview

Section 5 explores the configuration of Encrypted Filesystems and the encryption of Swap Space. Encryption is pivotal for safeguarding sensitive data, preventing unauthorized access, and securing information in case of hardware loss or theft.

Importance of Encryption

A. Purpose:

Encryption serves to:

- Prevent unauthorized access to sensitive data.

- Protect data in the event of hardware loss or theft.

Encrypting Filesystems and Swap Space

A. Setting Up Encrypted Filesystems:

1. Random Data Generation:

- Use `dd` to generate random data for enhanced security.

dd if=/dev/urandom of=/dev/sdb bs=4096

2. Install Cryptsetup:

- Update and install `cryptsetup` for managing encrypted volumes.

aptitude update && aptitude install cryptsetup

3. LUKS Format:

- Utilize `cryptsetup` to LUKS format the target partition (e.g., /dev/sdb1).

cryptsetup -y luksFormat /dev/sdb1

B. Encrypting Swap Space:

- Encrypting swap space enhances security.

Key Considerations and Best Practices

A. Partition Size Planning:

1. Careful Planning:

- Plan encrypted partition sizes thoughtfully as resizing can be time-consuming and pose a risk of data loss.

2. Regular Monitoring:

- Monitor partition usage regularly to prevent space exhaustion.

B. Encryption Best Practices:

1. Unique Encryption Keys:

- Use strong and unique keys for each encrypted partition.

CHAPTER 4: ESSENTIAL COMMANDS

Section 1: Processing Text Streams in Linux

Overview

Mastering the art of processing text streams in Linux is crucial for efficient system administration. Understanding the importance of text streams and utilizing essential command-line tools are vital components of this section.

Importance of Text Streams in Linux Systems

A. Significance:

Text streams in Linux play a pivotal role in system administration, allowing seamless processing and manipulation of data through command-line tools.

Essential Command-Line Tools for Text Stream Processing

A. Overview:

Several indispensable command-line tools facilitate efficient text stream processing. Key tools include:

1. tr (Translate or Delete):

- Translates or deletes characters.

Practical Examples of Text Stream Processing

A. Using grep:

- Searching for a specific word in a file using the grep command.

grep 'word' filename

B. Using awk:

- Printing the first column of a file using the awk command.

`awk '{print $1}' filename`

C. Using sed:

- Replacing all occurrences of a word in a file using the sed command.

`sed 's/old-word/new-word/g' filename`

D. Using tr:

- Converting the contents of a file to upper-case using the tr command.

`tr '[:lower:]' '[:upper:]' < filename`

Common Text Processing Tasks

A. Pattern Matching:

- Finding and possibly replacing patterns in a text stream. Tools like grep and sed excel in pattern matching.

B. Substitution:

- Replacing occurrences of a pattern within a text stream. Sed is commonly used for substitution.

C. Text Transformation:

- Operations like converting text case, translating characters, and deleting characters. Tools like tr and awk are go-to options for text transformation.

Best Practices for Text Stream Processing on Linux

A. Regular Expressions:

- Ensure correct regular expressions when using grep, awk, and sed.

B. Substitution Safety:

- Exercise caution when performing substitutions using sed; consider making a backup of the file.

C. Awk Operations:

- Understand that awk operates on a line-by-line basis, making multi-line operations tricky.

D. tr Considerations:

- Be mindful that tr works with ASCII values, necessitating awareness of the order of character sets.

Section 2: Learn Vi/Vim as a Full-Text Editor

Overview

Mastering Vi/Vim as a full-text editor is essential for efficient text manipulation and system administration tasks. Understanding the significance, fundamental concepts, essential commands, and advanced features of Vi/Vim contributes to success in this section.

Significance of Vi/Vim in Linux Systems

A. Importance:

Vi/Vim is a powerful and ubiquitous text editor in Linux, providing efficient text manipulation capabilities crucial for system administrators.

Fundamental Concepts of Modes in Vi/Vim

A. Normal Mode:

- Default mode for navigating and manipulating text.

B. Insert Mode:

- Used for inserting and editing text within the file.

Essential Vi/Vim Commands

A. Key Commands:

1. `i`: Enter insert mode.

2. `Esc`: Return to command mode.

3. `x` or `Del`: Delete a character.

4. `yy`: Copy a line.

5. `dd`: Delete a line.

6. `p`: Paste the content of the buffer.

7. `/`: Initiate search, with cycling through matches using `n` and `N`.

Practical Examples of Using Vi/Vim

A. Changing Capitalization in Vim:

- Example: To convert the last line to uppercase, use `:$norm gUU`.

B. Vim Search and Replace Tips:

- Example: Replace all occurrences of a word in a file with `:%s/old-word/new-word/g`.

Advanced Features of Vi/Vim

A. Auto-complete:

- Vim offers built-in auto-completion with Ctrl-n or Ctrl-p in insert mode.

B. Buffers:

- Vim allows working with multiple files simultaneously using buffers.

C. Recordings:

- Vim permits recording and playing back sequences of commands.

D. Visual Block Mode:

- Enables selecting text in a block-shaped manner.

E. Macros:

- Vim supports recording a series of commands as a macro for playback.

Best Practices for Using Vi/Vim

A. Regular Expressions:

- Ensure correctness when using regular expressions with tools like grep, awk, and sed.

B. Substitution Safety:

- Exercise caution and create backups before performing substitutions with sed.

C. Awk Operations:

- Remember that awk operates on a line-by-line basis, potentially impacting multi-line operations.

D. tr for Text Transformations:

- Be aware that tr works with ASCII values, requiring attention to the order of character sets.

Section 3: Learning Basic Shell Scripting and Troubleshooting

Overview

This section is dedicated to Basic Shell Scripting and Troubleshooting. It emphasizes the significance of shell scripting in Linux system administration and introduces fundamental concepts and best practices. Additionally, it provides systematic troubleshooting methodologies and strategies for identifying and resolving common problems.

Importance of Shell Scripting in Linux System Administration and Troubleshooting

A. Automation Impact:

- Shell scripting in Linux significantly automates tasks, leading to time savings and increased productivity for system administrators.

Basics of Shell Scripting

A. Key Elements:

1. Variables:

- Store and manipulate data within the script.

- Example:

myVar="Hello, World!"

2. Control Structures:

- Loops (for, while) and conditional statements (if, else) control script flow.

- Example:

```
for i in {1..5}; do
  echo "Iteration $i"
done
```

3. Functions:

- Reusable blocks of code performing specific tasks.

- Example:

```
myFunction() {
  echo "This is a function."
}
myFunction
```

Best Practices in Shell Scripting

A. Code Readability:

- Use meaningful variable and function names.

- Include comments to explain complex logic.

- Example:

This script does a specific task

B. Error Handling:

- Implement error checking to handle and report errors effectively.

- Example:

```
if [ ! -f "$file" ]; then
  echo "File not found: $file"
fi
```

C. Version Control:

- Utilize version control systems to track changes in scripts.

- Example:

git init

git add script.sh

git commit -m "Initial script version"

Troubleshooting in Linux Systems

A. Systematic Troubleshooting Methodologies:

- Follow systematic approaches for effective troubleshooting.

B. Strategies for Identifying and Resolving Common Problems:

1. Permissions:

- Use `ls -l` to view file or directory permissions.

- Example:

ls -l /path/to/file

2. Services:

- Employ `systemctl` to check service status.

- Restart services if not running as expected.

- Example:

systemctl status serviceName

systemctl restart serviceName

3. Configuration Files:

- Inspect configuration files for syntax errors or incorrect settings.

- Example:

nano /etc/configfile.conf

Section 4: Learn the Basics of Git to Manage Projects Efficiently

Overview

This section is dedicated to mastering the basics of Git, a version control system essential for efficient project management. Understanding fundamental Git concepts, processes, and best practices is crucial for success in this section.

Fundamental Concepts of Git

A. Repositories:

- A Git repository serves as a virtual storage for your project, tracking changes and versions.

- Example:

git init

B. Branches:

- Branches in Git are pointers to specific commits, allowing parallel development.

- Example:

git branch feature-branch

C. Commits:

- A commit represents an individual change to a file or a set of files.

- Example:

git commit -m "Implemented new feature"

Process of Using Git

1. Merging:

- Git merging integrates forked histories, combining different branches into a unified history.

- Example:

git merge feature-branch

Best Practices for Git Usage

A. Commit Messages:

- Commit messages should be clear, concise, and relevant to changes made.

- Example:

git commit -m "Fix issue with authentication"

B. Branching Strategies:

- Establish a clear branching strategy for efficient collaboration and feature development.

- Example:

git branch -d feature-branch

C. Handling Merge Conflicts:

- Merge conflicts should be resolved carefully to maintain code integrity.

- Example:

git merge main

Resolve conflicts

git commit -m "Merged changes with conflict resolution"

Collaboration with Remotes and Basic Git Workflows

A. Remotes:

- Collaboration is facilitated through remote repositories using commands like `git clone`, `git pull`, and `git push`.

- Example:

git clone remote_repository_url

B. Basic Git Workflows:

- Adopting workflows like feature branching and pull requests streamlines collaboration.

- Example:

git checkout -b new-feature

git commit -m "Implemented new feature"

git push origin new-feature

CHAPTER 5: USERS AND GROUPS

Section 1: Managing Users & Groups and Enabling sudo Access

Overview

Mastering user and group management, along with configuring sudo access, is vital for Linux System Administration. Understanding key commands and configurations is essential for success in this section.

Importance of User and Group Management in Linux System Administration

- Efficient user and group management ensures proper access control and security in Linux systems.

- Properly assigning permissions helps organize resources and enhances system security.

Key Aspects:

- **Access Control:** Regulating user access to resources.
- **Security:** Ensuring the confidentiality and integrity of data.
- **Resource Organization:** Structuring access based on roles and responsibilities.

Key Commands and Configuration Files for Managing Users and Groups

Managing Users

1. useradd: Adding a New User

The **useradd** command is used to add a new user to the system.

Syntax:

useradd username

2. usermod: Modifying User Attributes

The **usermod** command allows for the modification of user attributes.

Syntax:

usermod options username

3. userdel: Deleting a User

The **userdel** command is employed to delete a user from the system.

Syntax:

userdel username

Managing Groups

1. groupadd: Adding a New Group

The **groupadd** command is used to add a new group to the system.

Syntax:

groupadd groupname

2. groupmod: Modifying Group Attributes

The **groupmod** command facilitates the modification of group attributes.

Syntax:

groupmod options groupname

3. groupdel: Deleting a Group

The **groupdel** command deletes a group from the system.

Syntax:

groupdel groupname

Understanding Sudo (Superuser Do)

Sudo is a powerful tool that allows users to execute commands with superuser privileges while maintaining a secure audit trail.

Configuring Sudo Access for Users

To grant sudo access to a user, you can do any of the following:

1. Add him to the sudo group.

Example:

usermod -aG sudo username

2. Edit the sudoers file using `sudo visudo` for syntax validation.

Example:

Open the sudoers file. This can be done by running:

sudo visudo

In the opened file, you need to add a line for the user you want to grant sudo access to. The line should look like this:

<user> ALL=(ALL) ALL

Replace <user> with the username of the user you want to grant sudo access to. This line gives the user full sudo privileges, meaning they can run all commands as root.

If you want the user to run sudo commands without being asked for a password each time, you can add NOPASSWD: to the line:

<user> ALL=(ALL) NOPASSWD: ALL

Best Practices for User and Group Management

Maintaining a secure and organized system involves adhering to best practices.

Recommendations:

- Provide sudo access on a per-user or per-group basis.
- Regularly review and audit sudo access permissions for security.

Practical Examples

Apply the concepts learned in real-world scenarios.

1. User and Group Management:

- **Adding a user:**

useradd username

- **Modifying a user:**

usermod options username

- **Deleting a user:**

userdel username

- **Adding a user to a group:**

usermod -aG groupname username

2. Sudo Access Configuration:

- **Running a command with sudo:**

sudo command

- **Adding a user to the sudo group:**

usermod -aG sudo username

Section 2: Set Access Control Lists (ACLs) and Disk Quotas

Overview

This section emphasizes mastering Access Control Lists (ACLs) and implementing Disk Quotas. Understanding the syntax, practical usage, and best practices is crucial for effective system administration.

Access Control Lists (ACLs)

A. Syntax and Usage of ACL Commands:

The `setfacl` command is instrumental in managing ACLs, allowing fine-grained control over file and directory permissions.

Practical Examples of ACLs

Scenario: Accounting Department Directory

Suppose there is a directory dedicated to files from the accounting department. Set permissions to allow the accounting service user (user owner) and members of the accounting group (owner group) to read and write.

Allowing read and write for the user owner

```
setfacl -m u:accounting-service:rw /path/to/accounting-directory
```

Allowing read and write for the owner group

```
setfacl -m g:accounting-group:rw /path/to/accounting-directory
```

Disk Quotas

A. Setting Up and Enforcing Disk Quotas:

Use the `quota` and `edquota` commands to establish and enforce disk quotas. The `quota` command displays disk usage and limits, while `edquota` edits user quotas.

Practical Examples of Disk Quotas

Scenario: Shared Environment

Consider a shared environment like a web hosting or file server, allowing multiple users to connect and store data. Implement quotas to prevent individual users from consuming the entire disk space.

\# Displaying disk usage and limits for a user

```
quota -u username
```

\# Editing user quotas interactively

```
edquota username
```

Best Practices for Monitoring and Managing Disk Usage

- Regularly monitor disk usage using tools like `quota` to ensure compliance with allocated limits.

- Implement periodic reviews of ACL configurations to maintain security and access control.

- When assigning ACLs, provide the minimum necessary permissions to reduce security risks.

CHAPTER 6: INFORMATION RELEVANT TO MULTIPLE DOMAINS AND COMPETENCIES

Section 1: Archiving and Compression Tools / Basic File Permissions and Attributes

Overview

This section, we delve into Archiving and Compression Tools, as well as Basic File Permissions and Attributes. These skills are fundamental for efficient data management and security in Linux system administration.

Archiving and Compression Tools in Linux

Archiving and compression play a pivotal role in Linux system administration, addressing data security and storage efficiency. It is essential to choose the right tool based on factors like compression rate, data nature, and available computational resources.

Practical Examples:

1. Create a tar archive:

```
tar -cvf archive.tar /path/to/directory
```

2. Extract a tar archive:

```
tar -xvf archive.tar
```

3. Create a gzip compressed file:

```
gzip filename
```

4. Decompress a gzip file:

```
gunzip filename.gz
```

5. Create a zip archive:

zip archive.zip file1 file2 file3

6. Extract a zip archive:

unzip archive.zip

These examples showcase practical commands, empowering candidates to master archiving and compression techniques based on specific needs.

Basic File Permissions and Attributes in Linux

File security and access control are critical aspects of Linux system administration. Permissions, represented in octal notation, dictate who can read, write, and execute files. Ownership, involving user and group assignments, further refines access control. File attributes such as setuid, setgid, and the sticky bit enhance security measures.

Practical Examples:

1. Change the owner of a file:

chown newowner filename

2. Change the group of a file:

chgrp newgroup filename

3. Change permissions of a file:

chmod 755 filename

These practical examples demonstrate the manipulation of file ownership, group assignments, and permissions, providing a solid foundation for effective file management and security in Linux systems.

Section 2: Linux Help Documentations and Tools

Overview

In this section, we explore the intricacies of Linux Help Documentations and Tools, essential for mastering the skills required in Linux system administration.

Importance of Accurate Documentation and Efficient Tools in Linux System Administration

Accurate documentation and efficient tools are paramount in Linux system administration, providing a wealth of information about the system, its components, and their interactions. Proficiency in utilizing these resources is crucial for effective management and troubleshooting.

Various Sources of Linux Help Documentation

Linux offers diverse sources of help documentation, each serving a unique purpose. These resources empower administrators with insights into system architecture, configuration, and troubleshooting.

Essential Linux Command-Line Tools

Understanding key command-line tools is fundamental for efficient system management. Here are examples that every LFCS candidate should be familiar with:

1. top:

- Provides a dynamic real-time view of running processes.

- Example:

top

System Logs and Their Role in Troubleshooting

System logs play a pivotal role in troubleshooting and monitoring system health. The exact location and naming conventions of log files can vary, and familiarity with these details is crucial for effective log analysis.

Log Locations and Common Log Files

1. Log locations: Vary across distributions and software components.

2. Common log files: Examples include `/var/log/messages` and `/var/log/syslog`.

Using journalctl for Accessing Log Information

1. journalctl:

- A tool for accessing log information.

- Example:

journalctl

Interpreting Log Entries and Identifying Potential Issues

Understanding log entries is vital for identifying and resolving issues. LFCS candidates should be adept at interpreting logs to troubleshoot effectively.

Section 3: Configure and Troubleshoot Grand Unified Boot-loader (GRUB)

Overview

In this section, we delve into the intricacies of configuring and troubleshooting the Grand Unified Boot-loader (GRUB), a critical component of the Linux boot process.

Role of GRUB in the Linux Boot Process

GRUB plays a pivotal role in the Linux boot process, acting as the bootloader responsible for loading the operating system. It facilitates the selection of the kernel and initial RAM disk, initiating the boot sequence.

By default, the GRUB configuration file (`/etc/default/grub`) includes the line `GRUB_DEFAULT=0`, indicating that the first entry in the GRUB menu is set as the default. This default setting can be adjusted based on the desired boot entry index.

Troubleshooting Common GRUB-related Issues

Common GRUB-related issues encompass boot failures, incorrect configurations, or missing boot entries. Knowledge of GRUB basics and its configuration is instrumental in interpreting error messages and resolving these issues effectively.

Understanding the key commands and parameters in the GRUB shell can aid in troubleshooting. For instance, to manually boot a specific kernel, candidates can use the following GRUB commands:

```
grub> set root=(hd0,1)   # Set the root partition
```

```
grub> linux /vmlinuz-<kernel-version> root=/dev/sda1   # Specify the
kernel and root partition
```

```
grub> initrd /initrd.img-<kernel-version>   # Specify the initial RAM
disk
```

```
grub> boot   # Initiate the boot process
```

Section 4: Monitor Linux Processes Resource Usage

Overview

In this section, we delve into the critical task of monitoring Linux processes and their resource usage, focusing on essential command-line tools for effective system monitoring.

Essential Linux Command-Line Tools for Process Monitoring

Linux provides a range of commands and tools to facilitate comprehensive system monitoring. Here are key tools that every LFCS candidate should be proficient in:

1. top:

- Provides a dynamic real-time view of running processes.

- Example:

`top`

2. htop:

- An interactive system monitor supporting scrolling and mouse interaction.

- Example:

`htop`

These tools empower administrators to gain insights into system resource utilization, aiding in proactive monitoring and issue identification.

Understanding Signals and Terminating Processes

Signals allow the operating system to communicate with processes. The termination of processes is a crucial aspect of system management.

Terminating Processes Using the kill Command

The `kill` command in Linux is used to terminate processes gracefully. Understanding the syntax and options of the `kill` command is essential for effectively managing processes.

- Example: To gracefully terminate a process with a specific process ID (PID):

kill PID

- Example: To forcefully terminate a process:

kill -9 PID

Section 5: Setting Up FTP Server to Allow Anonymous Logins

Overview

In this section, we explore the process of configuring an FTP server to permit anonymous logins, a crucial aspect of Linux system administration.

Setting Up an FTP Server

To establish an FTP server, it is imperative to install the necessary components. This ensures that the server is equipped to handle file transfers seamlessly.

Configuring FTP Server for Anonymous Logins

After the installation of essential components, the FTP server must be configured to permit anonymous logins. This step involves adjusting configuration files to enable anonymous access.

Relevant Configuration Files and Permissions

FTP server configuration entails managing various files and permissions to ensure proper functionality. Understanding the significance of these files is essential for successful FTP server deployment.

Practical Examples

Let's consider a simplified example of setting up an anonymous FTP directory on a Linux server using `vsftpd`:

1. Install vsftpd and ftp:

Use the package manager of your Linux distribution to install the necessary packages.

```
sudo apt-get install vsftpd ftp  # Example for Debian/Ubuntu
```

2. Edit vsftpd.conf file:

Modify the `vsftpd.conf` file to enable anonymous logins.

```
sudo nano /etc/vsftpd.conf
```

3. Create a directory for anonymous FTP:

```
sudo mkdir /srv/ftp
```

4. Set appropriate permissions for the anonymous FTP directory:

```
sudo chown -R ftp:ftp /srv/ftp
sudo chmod -R 755 /srv/ftp
```

Security Considerations and Best Practices

While anonymous logins provide convenience, they pose security risks. Implementing security measures is crucial to safeguard the system:

Permissions and Restrictions

Maintaining system security involves implementing appropriate permissions and restrictions. Striking a balance between accessibility and security is crucial for effective FTP server management.

Section 6: Installation and Configuration of MariaDB Database Server

Overview

In this section, we explore the comprehensive process of installing and configuring MariaDB, a robust and popular choice for a database server in Linux system administration.

Importance of Database Servers in Linux System Administration

Database servers play a pivotal role in Linux system administration, serving as essential components for storing and managing data efficiently.

Installing MariaDB on a Linux System

Follow this simplified step-by-step process to install MariaDB on a Linux system:

1. Update your package index:

Use the appropriate command based on your distribution:

- For Debian/Ubuntu:

`sudo apt update`

- For Red Hat/Fedora:

`sudo yum update`

OR

`sudo dnf update`

2. Install MariaDB:

Use the package manager to install MariaDB:

- For Debian/Ubuntu:

`sudo apt install mariadb-server`

- For Red Hat/Fedora:

`sudo yum install mariadb-server`

OR

`sudo dnf install mariadb-server`

3. Start MariaDB service:

After installation, initiate the MariaDB service:

`sudo systemctl start mariadb.service`

Initial Configuration of MariaDB

Securing the MariaDB installation is crucial post-installation to prevent unauthorized access and enhance overall security.

Essential MariaDB Configuration Files

MariaDB configuration involves key files, with `my.cnf` being central to optimizing database operations. Editing this file allows administrators to tweak parameters for better performance.

Optimizing Database Operations

Tweaking parameters in the `my.cnf` file is vital for optimizing MariaDB database operations. This involves adjusting settings such as cache sizes, query execution parameters, and thread configurations.

User Management within MariaDB

Effective user management in MariaDB involves utilizing SQL commands for creating databases, tables, and user accounts. Examples of SQL commands include:

- Create a database:

SQL

CREATE DATABASE mydatabase;

- Create a table:

SQL

CREATE TABLE mytable (column1 INT, column2 VARCHAR(255));

- Create a user:

SQL

CREATE USER 'username'@'localhost' IDENTIFIED BY 'password';

Securing MariaDB Databases

Security best practices for MariaDB include granting minimal necessary permissions, using strong passwords, and regularly updating and patching the software.

Section 7: Setup Apache SSL with Name-Based Virtual Hosting

Overview

In this section, we explore the configuration of Apache SSL with Name-Based Virtual Hosting, focusing on the importance of securing web traffic using SSL/TLS protocols.

Significance of Securing Web Traffic Using SSL/TLS Protocols

SSL (Secure Sockets Layer) and its successor, TLS (Transport Layer Security), play a crucial role in securing communication between the web server and the client. This ensures the protection of sensitive information during transmission. To achieve this:

1. Installation of Necessary SSL Modules:

Install the required SSL modules for Apache, ensuring that the server is equipped to handle secure connections. Depending on your distribution:

- For Debian/Ubuntu:

```
sudo apt install apache2 openssl
sudo a2enmod ssl
sudo systemctl restart apache2
```

- For Red Hat/Fedora:

```
sudo yum install httpd mod_ssl
sudo systemctl restart httpd
```

Configuring Apache to Serve Different Websites on the Same IP Address Using Server Name Indication (SNI)

Apache can be configured to serve multiple websites on the same IP address using Server Name Indication (SNI). This allows the server to distinguish between different virtual hosts based on the requested domain.

- Example Apache Virtual Host Configuration with SNI:

```
<VirtualHost :443>
  ServerName example.com
  DocumentRoot /var/www/example
  SSLEngine on
  SSLCertificateFile /etc/ssl/certs/example.com.crt
  SSLCertificateKeyFile /etc/ssl/private/example.com.key
</VirtualHost>
```

Best Practices for SSL Certificate Management

Effective SSL certificate management is crucial for maintaining web server security. Adopt the following best practices:

- Regularly review SSL protocols and settings.

- Keep track of certificate expiry dates and renew certificates before expiration.

- Regularly update and monitor SSL/TLS configurations.

- Implement strong security practices and continuous education and awareness.

Section 8: Setup an Iptables Firewall

Overview

In this section, we delve into the crucial task of setting up and managing an Iptables firewall, focusing on the role of firewalls in securing Linux systems.

Role of Firewalls in Securing Linux Systems

Firewalls play a fundamental role in enhancing the security of Linux systems by regulating incoming and outgoing network traffic. They act as barriers that filter and control data flow, preventing unauthorized access and potential security threats.

Basics of Iptables

Iptables is a powerful tool for configuring the Linux kernel's built-in firewall. It allows administrators to define rules for packet filtering, network address translation, and packet mangling. Understanding the basics of Iptables is essential for effective firewall management.

Setting Up Iptables

Configuring Iptables involves defining rules to specify how the firewall should handle different types of network traffic. Here's a simplified example of setting up Iptables to allow SSH (port 22) and HTTP (port 80) traffic while blocking all other incoming connections:

```
sudo iptables -A INPUT -p tcp --dport 22 -j ACCEPT   # Allow SSH

sudo iptables -A INPUT -p tcp --dport 80 -j ACCEPT   # Allow HTTP

sudo iptables -A INPUT -j DROP       # Drop all other incoming
```

connections

Practical Examples of Common Iptables Configurations

1. Allowing specific IP address:

sudo iptables -A INPUT -s <trusted_ip> -j ACCEPT

2. Blocking specific IP address:

sudo iptables -A INPUT -s <untrusted_ip> -j DROP

3. Port forwarding:

sudo iptables -t nat -A PREROUTING -p tcp --dport 8080 -j DNAT --to-destination <internal_ip>:80

Iptables Persistence

To ensure that Iptables rules persist across reboots, use tools like `iptables-persistent` on Debian/Ubuntu or `iptables-service` on Red Hat/Fedora:

sudo apt-get install iptables-persistent   # For Debian/Ubuntu

sudo systemctl enable iptables.service   # For Red Hat/Fedora

Logging and Monitoring Firewall Activity

Considerations for logging and monitoring firewall activity are critical for identifying potential security threats. Iptables can log packets and their status. Example for logging dropped packets:

sudo iptables -A INPUT -j LOG --log-prefix "Dropped: "

Section 9: System Usage, Utilization, and Troubleshooting

Overview

In this section, we delve into the critical aspects of System Usage, Utilization, and Troubleshooting, emphasizing the importance of monitoring system performance and understanding resource utilization.

Importance of Monitoring System Performance, Understanding Resource Utilization, and Troubleshooting

Monitoring system performance is pivotal for maintaining the stability and efficiency of a Linux system. Understanding resource utilization enables administrators to identify potential bottlenecks and optimize system performance. Troubleshooting skills are essential for identifying and resolving issues that may arise in the system.

Essential Linux Commands and Tools for Monitoring System Usage

1. top:

- Provides a dynamic real-time view of the processes running in the system.

- Example:

```
top
```

2. vmstat:

- Monitors Linux system's memory and CPU usage over time.

- Example:

vmstat

3. sar (System Activity Reporter):

- Collects and reports system activity information.

- Example:

sar -u

4. iostat:

- Reports statistics about disk input and output operations and CPU utilization.

- Example:

iostat -xz

System Utilization Metrics and Identification of Potential Bottlenecks

System utilization metrics offer insights into resource usage patterns. Identifying potential bottlenecks allows administrators to proactively address issues and optimize system performance.

Strategies for Optimizing System Performance

Optimizing system performance involves various strategies, including:

- Adjusting process priorities.

- Managing memory usage.

- Optimizing disk I/O.

- Tuning network parameters.

Troubleshooting in Linux Systems

Troubleshooting encompasses the identification and resolution of issues that may impact system performance. Effective troubleshooting skills are vital for maintaining a robust and reliable Linux system.

Practical Examples

1. High CPU Usage:

- Use `top` to identify resource-consuming processes.

- Example:

```
top
```

2. Slow Response Times:

- Use `vmstat` and `iostat` to monitor disk I/O operations.

- Example:

```
vmstat
```

```
iostat -xz
```

Real-world Application of Monitoring Tools and Troubleshooting Techniques

In scenarios such as high CPU usage or slow response times, monitoring tools like `top`, `vmstat`, and `iostat` can be applied for effective troubleshooting. For instance, identifying resource-intensive processes with `top` helps pinpoint performance bottlenecks, enabling further investigation and optimization.

Section 10: Setting up a Network Repository

Overview

In this section, we explore the intricacies of setting up a Network Repository, covering both the initial setup and maintenance aspects.

Setting Up a Network Repository

The process of setting up a network repository involves the following essential steps:

1. Installation and Configuration of Server Software:

- Install and configure the necessary server software, such as Apache or Nginx, to serve as the platform for hosting the network repository.

- Example (using Apache):

sudo apt update

sudo apt install apache2

sudo systemctl start apache2

2. Selection of a Repository Management Tool:

- Choose a repository management tool like `apt-mirror` for Debian/Ubuntu or `createrepo` for RPM-based distributions. These tools facilitate the management and synchronization of the repository.

- Example (using apt-mirror):

sudo apt install apt-mirror

Troubleshooting and Monitoring

Common issues related to network repositories may include synchronization problems or client configuration errors. Resolve these issues by checking configuration settings and ensuring client systems are correctly set up to use the network repository.

1. Checking Repository Synchronization:

- Example (using apt-mirror):

```
sudo apt-mirror
```

2. Verifying Client Configuration:

- Ensure clients are configured to access the repository correctly.

- Example (updating apt source list):

```
sudo echo "deb http://repository_server/ubuntu focal main" >> /etc/apt/sources.list
sudo apt update
```

Monitoring Repository Health

Monitoring the repository's health is crucial for efficient software distribution and management in Linux systems. Ensure reliable access for client systems by implementing regular checks.

1. Monitoring Repository Status:

- Regularly check the repository's status to ensure synchronization and availability.

- Example:

```
systemctl status apache2
```

2. Access Testing from Client Systems:

- Verify client systems can access the repository.

- Example:

```
curl -I http://repository_server
```

Section 11: Network Performance, Security, and Troubleshooting

Overview

In this section, we explore the critical aspects of Network Performance, Security, and Troubleshooting, emphasizing the significance of a well-optimized and secure network in Linux systems.

Importance of Network Performance and Security

A well-performing and secure network is paramount for the efficiency and reliability of Linux systems. Monitoring and optimizing network performance ensure smooth data flow, while robust security measures safeguard against common network threats, fostering a resilient network infrastructure.

Monitoring Network Performance

Monitoring network performance involves the use of various tools and techniques to assess and enhance data transfer capabilities. Essential tools include:

1. iperf:
- Measures network bandwidth performance.
- Example:

```
iperf -s  # On the server
iperf -c <server_ip>  # On the client
```

2. Wireshark:
- Analyzes network traffic for diagnostics.

- Example:

wireshark

Network Security

Securing a Linux network is crucial for protecting sensitive data and ensuring the integrity of communication. Security measures include:

1. iptables:

- Controls network traffic by setting up rules.

- Example (allowing SSH traffic):

sudo iptables -A INPUT -p tcp --dport 22 -j ACCEPT

2. Intrusion Detection System (IDS):

- Monitors for suspicious activities on the network.

- Example:

  - Installing Snort:

  sudo apt-get install snort

Troubleshooting Network Issues

Troubleshooting network issues is a critical skill for Linux administrators. Diagnose and resolve problems using techniques such as:

1. Ping and Traceroute:

- Identify connectivity and routing issues.

- Example (pinging a host):

ping <host_ip>

2. Netstat:

- Displays network connections, routing tables, interface statistics, masquerade connections, and more.

- Example:

`netstat -a`

Practical Examples

In real-world scenarios, administrators might employ iperf to assess bandwidth, Wireshark for in-depth traffic analysis, set up iptables rules to control traffic flow, or configure an IDS like Snort to monitor for suspicious activities.

EPILOGUE

As we reach the end of "Mastering LFCS: Your Gateway to Linux Certification," my hope is that this book has served as a valuable resource in your journey towards Linux mastery. The path to becoming a Linux Foundation Certified System Administrator is not an easy one, but it is a journey filled with immense learning and growth.

The world of Linux is vast and ever-evolving, and the knowledge you have gained through this book is just the beginning. As you continue to explore, remember that the true essence of mastery lies not just in the understanding of the system but also in the curiosity to learn more.

Whether you are preparing for the LFCS exam or seeking to enhance your skills in Linux system administration, remember that every challenge you overcome, every problem you solve, and every command you master brings you one step closer to your goal.

As you close this book, you are not ending your journey but embarking on a new phase. A phase where you apply your knowledge, explore new frontiers, and continue to master the art of Linux.

Here's to your success in the LFCS exam and your continued journey in the world of Linux!

Ghada Atef

ABOUT THE AUTHOR

Ghada Atef

Ghada Atef is a seasoned Linux expert with a passion for open-source technologies. With a deep understanding of various Linux distributions and their applications, she has authored several comprehensive guides and practice exams to help aspiring Linux professionals.

Her works include:

1. "Unofficial Red Hat RHCSA 9 (EX200) Exam Preparation 2023: Six Complete RHCSA 9 (EX200) Practice Exams with Answers (Third Edition)" - The third edition of the comprehensive guide to the RHCSA 9 (EX200) exam, featuring six complete practice exams.
2. "Mastering Ansible: A Comprehensive Guide to Automating Configuration Management and Deployment" - A detailed exploration of Ansible, providing practical knowledge on automating configuration management and deployment.
3. "Mastering Ubuntu: A Comprehensive Guide to Linux's Favorite" - An in-depth guide to using and mastering Ubuntu, one of the most popular Linux distributions.
4. "Unofficial Red Hat Certified System Administrator RHCSA 8 & 9 (EX200) Exam Preparation 2023: Six Complete RHCSA 8 & 9 Practice Exams with Answers" - A thorough preparation guide for the RHCSA 8 & 9 (EX200) exam, featuring six complete practice

exams.

5. "RHCE EX294 Mastery: Six Practice Exams for Exam Success" - A comprehensive guide offering detailed answers to ace the Red Hat Certified Engineer EX294 Exam.

6. "Unofficial Red Hat RHCSA 9 (EX200) Exam Preparation 2023: Master the Red Hat RHCSA 9 (EX200) Exam with Confidence" - An online course designed to build confidence and knowledge for the RHCSA 9 (EX200) exam.

Ghada's work is characterized by its practical approach, clear explanations, and real-world relevance. Her dedication to helping others master Linux is evident in the depth and breadth of her work. Whether you're a beginner just starting out or a seasoned professional looking to validate your skills, Ghada's books and courses are an invaluable resource on your journey.

BOOKS BY THIS AUTHOR

Unofficial Rhcsa 8 & 9 (Ex200) Complete Reference: Rhel 8 & 9

"Unofficial RHCSA 8 & 9 (EX200) Complete Reference: RHEL 8 & 9" is a comprehensive guide that covers all the topics and objectives of the Red Hat Certified System Administrator (RHCSA) exam for RHEL 8 and 9. Whether you're a beginner or an experienced Linux user, this book provides you with the knowledge and skills to become proficient in managing and maintaining RHEL systems. From installation and configuration to system management, networking, security, and troubleshooting, this book covers everything you need to know to pass the RHCSA exam and become a certified system administrator. With clear explanations, practical examples, and real-world scenarios, "Unofficial RHCSA 8 & 9 (EX200) Complete Reference: RHEL 8 & 9" is an essential resource for anyone preparing for the RHCSA exam or seeking to improve their RHEL skills.

Mastering Ansible: A Comprehensive Guide To Automating Configuration Management And Deployment

"Mastering Ansible: A Comprehensive Guide to Automating Configuration Management and Deployment" is an in-depth guide to Ansible, a popular open-source tool for automating infrastructure as code.

The book covers everything from the basics of Ansible to advanced topics such as modules, plugins, roles, and dynamic inventory. It provides detailed guidance on how to write efficient, modular, and reusable playbooks, and how to use Ansible to automate a wide range of tasks, from provisioning servers to deploying applications.

The book also includes best practices, tips, and tricks for working effectively with Ansible, as well as use cases and real-world examples.

Whether you're a beginner or an experienced user, "Mastering Ansible" will help you become a master of Ansible and take your automation skills to the next level.

Unofficial Red Hat Certified Engineer (Rhce) Ex294 Exam Guide: A Comprehensive Study Resource For Red Hat Enterprise Linux 9

Looking to become a Red Hat Certified Engineer (RHCE)? Look no further than "Unofficial Red Hat Certified Engineer (RHCE) EX294 Exam Guide"! This comprehensive study resource is designed to help you pass the RHCE EX294 exam with ease, providing in-depth coverage of all exam objectives and six complete practice exams to help you sharpen your skills. With its clear explanations, helpful tips, and real-world scenarios, this book is an essential tool for anyone looking to succeed on the RHCE EX294 exam and take their Linux skills to the next level. So why wait? Get your copy today and start preparing for exam success!

Mastering Ubuntu: A Comprehensive Guide To Linux's Favorite Distribution

Looking to master one of the most popular Linux distributions around? Look no further than "Mastering Ubuntu"! This comprehensive guide takes you on a journey from beginner to expert, with step-by-step tutorials and practical examples to help you get the most out of your Ubuntu system. Whether you're a developer, sysadmin, or just a curious user, "Mastering Ubuntu" has everything you need to take your skills to the next level. From installation and configuration to networking, security, and beyond, this book is your ultimate resource for mastering Ubuntu.

Learn Pycharm Ide For Kids: Using Pycharm Python Ide Community Edition

Looking for a fun and engaging way to introduce your child to the world of programming? Look no further than "Learn PyCharm IDE for Kids: Using PyCharm Python IDE Community Edition." This book offers a comprehensive guide to the PyCharm Python IDE, one of the most popular tools for programming in Python. With clear and easy-to-follow instructions, your child will learn how to use PyCharm to write and run Python code, as well as how to debug and troubleshoot their programs. Whether your child is a complete beginner or has some programming experience, "Learn PyCharm IDE for Kids" is the perfect resource to help them take their coding skills to the next level.

Unofficial Red Hat Rhcsa 9 (Ex200) Exam Preparation 2023: Six Complete Rhcsa 9 (Ex200) Practice Exams With Answers (Third Edition)

Looking to ace the Red Hat RHCSA 9 (EX200) exam? Look no further than the "Unofficial Red Hat RHCSA 9 (EX200) Exam Preparation 2023" book. With six complete practice exams for RHCSA 9, this book is the ultimate study resource for anyone preparing to take the RHCSA exam. Whether you're a beginner or an experienced professional, these practice exams will test your knowledge and skills, giving you the confidence you need to pass the RHCSA exam with flying colors. With answers and detailed explanations included, you'll be able to review and strengthen your understanding of key concepts, commands, and techniques. Don't take the RHCSA exam without this essential study guide!

Rhce Ex294 Mastery: Six Practice Exams For Exam Success

This book, "RHCE EX294 Mastery: Six Practice Exams for Exam Success," is your comprehensive guide to achieving RHCE certification. It provides the tools, strategies, and in-depth knowledge to confidently ace the RHCE EX294 exam and establish yourself as a true RHEL expert.

Command Line Mastery

A Comprehensive Guide to Linux and Bash: 615 MCQs with detailed explanations on Filesystem, Process Management, Permissions, Networking, and Bash Scripting

Master Lfcs 2024: Unleash Your Potential: Six Comprehensive Practice Exams With Detailed Answers For The Linux Foundation Certified System Administrator Exam

Master LFCS 2024: Unleash Your Potential" is your ultimate guide to acing the Linux Foundation Certified System Administrator Exam. With six comprehensive practice exams and detailed answers, this book is designed to equip you with the knowledge and skills needed to excel in Linux administration. Whether you're a beginner or a seasoned professional, this book will help you unlock your potential and rise to new heights in your career. Dive into the world of Linux with "Master LFCS 2024: Unleash Your Potential" and transform your learning journey into a successful certification achievement. Perfect for those seeking practical, comprehensive, and up-to-date study material for the

LFCS exam. Start your journey towards mastery today!

THANK YOU!